W0037614

ARTIFICIAL NEURAL NETWORK TRAINING AND SOFTWARE IMPLEMENTATION TECHNIQUES

COMPUTER NETWORKS

Additional books in this series can be found on Nova's website
under the Series tab.

COMPUTER NETWORKS

ARTIFICIAL NEURAL NETWORK TRAINING AND SOFTWARE IMPLEMENTATION TECHNIQUES

ALI KATTAN
ROSNI ABDULLAH
AND
ZONG WOO GEEM

Nova Science Publishers, Inc.
New York

Copyright ©2011 by Nova Science Publishers, Inc.

For permission to use material from this book please contact us:
Telephone 631-231-7269; Fax 631-231-8175
Web Site: http://www.novapublishers.com

NOTICE TO THE READER

The Publisher has taken reasonable care in the preparation of this book, but makes no expressed or implied warranty of any kind and assumes no responsibility for any errors or omissions. No liability is assumed for incidental or consequential damages in connection with or arising out of information contained in this book. The Publisher shall not be liable for any special, consequential, or exemplary damages resulting, in whole or in part, from the readers' use of, or reliance upon, this material. Any parts of this book based on government reports are so indicated and copyright is claimed for those parts to the extent applicable to compilations of such works.

Independent verification should be sought for any data, advice or recommendations contained in this book. In addition, no responsibility is assumed by the publisher for any injury and/or damage to persons or property arising from any methods, products, instructions, ideas or otherwise contained in this publication.

This publication is designed to provide accurate and authoritative information with regard to the subject matter covered herein. It is sold with the clear understanding that the Publisher is not engaged in rendering legal or any other professional services. If legal or any other expert assistance is required, the services of a competent person should be sought. FROM A DECLARATION OF PARTICIPANTS JOINTLY ADOPTED BY A COMMITTEE OF THE AMERICAN BAR ASSOCIATION AND A COMMITTEE OF PUBLISHERS.

LIBRARY OF CONGRESS CATALOGING-IN-PUBLICATION DATA

Kattan, Ali.
  Artificial neural network training and software implementation techniques / Ali Kattan, Rosni Abdullah, and Zong Woo Geem.
    p. cm.
  Includes bibliographical references and index.
  ISBN 978-1-61122-990-5 (softcover)
  1. Neural networks (Computer science) I. Abdullah, Rosni. II. Geem, Zong Woo. III. Title.
  QA76.87.K396 2011
  006.3'2--dc22
                         2011003231

Published by Nova Science Publishers, Inc. † New York

CONTENTS

PREFACE

Artificial neural networks (ANN) are widely used in diverse fields of science and industry. Though there have been numerous techniques used for their implementations, the choice of a specific implementation is subjected to different factors including cost, accuracy, processing speed and overall performance. Featured with synaptic plasticity, the process of training is concerned with adjusting the individual weights between each of the individual ANN neurons until we can achieve close to the desired output. Regardless of the implementation hardware, it is always preferable to have soft network architecture in the early stages of application development. This would facilitate the process of rapidly modifying the network's size and learning method. Software simulation on conventional computers is usually used as a measure of performance to compare with other approaches for ANN implementations. This book introduces the common trajectory-driven and evolutionary-based training algorithms. Implementation considers the use of cost effective techniques that is based on commodity hardware including implementations using graphical processing units (GPU) and parallel heterogeneous systems.

Chapter 1

INTRODUCTION

The work on Artificial Neural Networks (ANNs) began back in the 1950's motivated by a desire to try both to understand the human brain as well as to emulate some of its strengths. The degree in which an ANN models a certain biological neural system varies (Fausett, 1994). It could be the primary concern for some researchers to emulate such a biological system like simulation of a cortex (Johansson & Lansner, 2006), while for others the main interest is to mimic some of the useful tasks performed by this system such as controlling a robot (Jung & Kim, 2007).

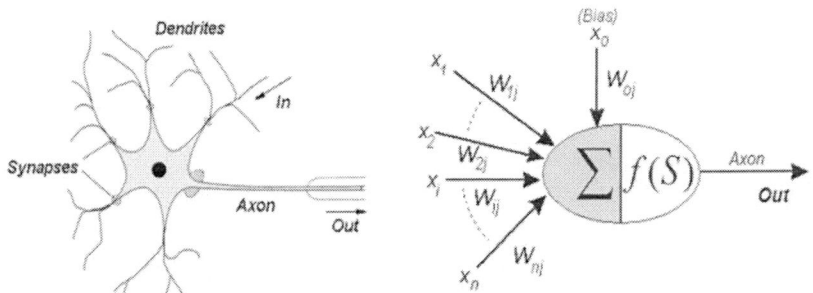

Figure 1. Generic biological neuron vs. classical artificial neuron representation.

The artificial neuron unit is fundamental to the operation of an ANN. Figure 1 shows a generic biological neuron versus a schematic representation of an artificial neuron. The input signals in this representation are continuous variables, which are not discrete electrical pulses like that of the brain (Padhy, 2005). Neurological research has showed that real biological neural networks use pulse-coding for the neuron output, where the information are encoded in the form of a sequence of spikes (Thorpe, Delorme & Van Rullen, 2001). ANN models based on the latter are referred to as spiking ANNs. A distinction is made between spiking and non-spiking ANNs where the former is usually referred to as the 3rd generation to distinguish it from the previous generations which are referred to as classical (Wang *et al.*, 2008).

In general one ANN model is not necessarily better than the other. It is the level of abstraction that is the main difference between them. In some models, all the biochemical aspects of the biological neuron are to be simulated accurately. The aim of such models is usually to deeply understand the functionality of biological neural networks such as the study of epilepsy (Hereld *et al.*, 2004). Some other models are much more abstract to the extent that some of them represent each neuron by just a real number called its activation (Ruf & Schmitt, 1998). Since this book is concerned with the classical ANN implementations only, the term ANN and neuron are used from now onwards to refer to those of the classical model.

With neurons as the basic building blocks, ANNs are developed as generalizations of mathematical models of human neural biology. They can be designed to be insensitive to small damage to the network. One of the most important characteristics of ANNs is the relatively high degree of fault tolerance (El Emam *et al.*, 1991). ANNs represent a computational paradigm, whose characteristics include intrinsic parallelism, local processing in neurons, distributed memory represented by weights and learning and recall modes (Mathia & Clark, 2002). As general taxonomy, an ANN is usually characterized by an architecture or topology, a certain activation function used in its neurons and a learning algorithm, (Fiesler & Beale, 1996). The topology of a neural network is a combination of its framework (the neurons) and its interconnection scheme. The layered or clustered structure is exhibited in most ANNs even biological ones. Fiesler (1994) showed that for universality all ANNs could be regarded as clustered. In most ANN architectures the neurons are clustered into layers, or more generally into slabs where a slab is a collection of neurons having similar function and hierarchical level.

Chapter 2

FEED-FORWARD NEURAL NETWORKS

A special class of ANNs is the multi-layer feed-forward ANN (FFANN) also known as multilayer or multiple-layer perceptron (MLP). During the past decades, this class of ANNs has achieved increased popularity among engineers, scientists as well as other professionals as tools for knowledge representation (Liang, 2007). The following sections would address the main characteristics of this type of ANNs.

2.1. TOPOLOGY

FFANNs are fully connected ANNs where each neuron in layer i is connected to all neurons in layer $i+1$ for all i (Montana & Davis, 1989) as shown in Figure 2. They are characterized by a topology that has no closed paths where no lateral connections exist between neurons in a given layer or back to the previous layers. The first layer of a FFANN is known as the input layer, the last layer is known as the output layer and the in-between layers are known as the hidden layers (Svozil, Kvasnicka & Pospichal, 1997; Padhy, 2005). Biases are considered as special weights fed with the value of -1 as an input signal.

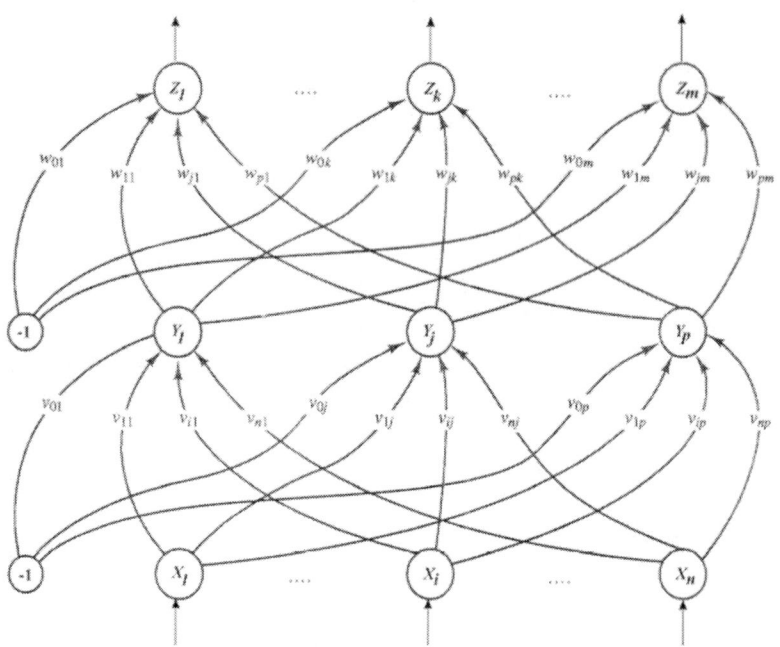

Figure 2. A multi layer feed-forward artificial neural network (FFANN).

FFANNs having a topology of just a single hidden layer, which sometimes referred to as 3-layer FFANNs, are considered as universal approximators for arbitrary finite-input environment measures (Bishop, 1999; Jiang & Wah, 2003; Marini, Magri & Bucci, 2007). Such configuration has proved its ability to match very complex patterns due to its capability to learn by example using relatively simple set of computations (Lane & Neidinger, 1995). Such FFANN topology is usually indicated by three numbers separated by dashes (X-H-Y) where X, H, and Y represent the number of units in the input, hidden and output layers respectively.

The number of inputs and outputs is usually governed by the problem's data set. The number of hidden neurons however is a design issue and is usually decided on the basis of experience (Yuan, Xiong & Huai, 2003). Yet, there have been many works that presented some formalism to estimate the best number of hidden units or set a lower and upper bound for such number based on different criteria (Fausett, 1994; Fujita, 1998; Teoh, Tan & Xiang, 2006).

Since this book is concerned with FFANNs having single hidden layer topology, the term FFANN would be used to refer to such networks from now onwards.

2.2. FUNCTIONALITY, PATTERN-RECOGNITION & FORECASTING

In general, ANNs have the main advantage of being able to use some priori unknown information hidden in data where they can realize an arbitrary mapping between one vector space onto another vector space (Svozil, Kvasnicka & Pospichal, 1997). When FFANNs are trained on a relatively sparse set of sample data points, referred to as training set, they often provide the right output for an out-of-sample input that is not in the training set (Montana & Davis, 1989). The process of training is concerned with adjusting the individual weights between each of the individual ANN neurons until we can achieve the close to the desired output. This FFANN training concept and the different training paradigms will be discussed thoroughly in chapter 4, 5 and 6.

Due to this learning capability, FFANNs became very popular and powerful tools that are used to solve a variety of complex problems. Applications like medical image screening, fingerprint identification and hand-written digit recognition are just few to mention (Bishop, 1999). In general there are two broad categories of such FFANN tools: pattern-recognition (also known as pattern-classification) tools and forecasting or prediction tools where a distinction is made between the two based on how the network's output is interpreted.

Pattern-classification networks would usually have more than one output unit in its output layer to designate "classes" or "groups" belonging to a certain type (Fiesler & Fulcher, 1994; Jiang & Wah, 2003). The unit that produces the highest output among other units would indicate the winning class, a technique that is known the "winner-take-all" (Fausett, 1994; Oh & Suen, 2002).

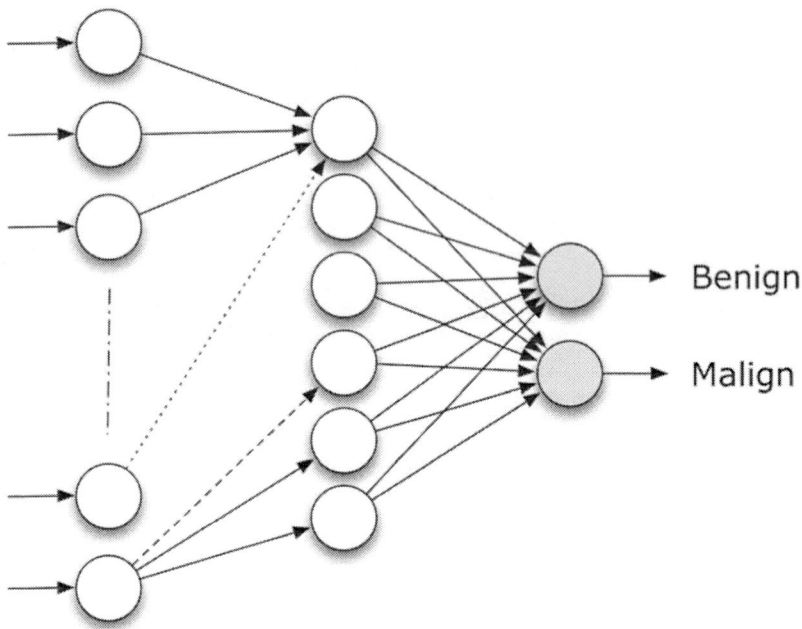

Figure 3. Pattern-Classifier 9-6-2 FFANN for breast cancer type.

Figure 3 shows an example of a pattern-classification problem that uses a 9-6-2 architecture. This network is used to detect the type of breast cancer being either "Benign" or "Malign" (Blum & Socha, 2005; Alba & Chicano, 2004). An output unit is dedicated for each cancer type or "class" and depending on the input data used, the network would classify this input as one of these classes indicated by the higher output value for the associated output unit. Character recognition applications are another common example for this type of pattern-classification networks such as the recognition of handwritten digits, English capital letters and Korean "Hangul" characters in postal addresses where these networks would have 10, 26 and 352 output units respectively (Oh & Suen, 2002).

Forecasting or prediction networks are characterized by having a single unit in the output layer where the real-valued output signal is interpreted based on its magnitude. Many decision support systems are based on this type of FFANN like engineering assessment applications (Geem, 2003; Geem et al., 2007). However, such networks can also be used for binary classification problems where the output would represent the probability that a case should be classified as "Yes" or "No" (Hassoun, 1995).

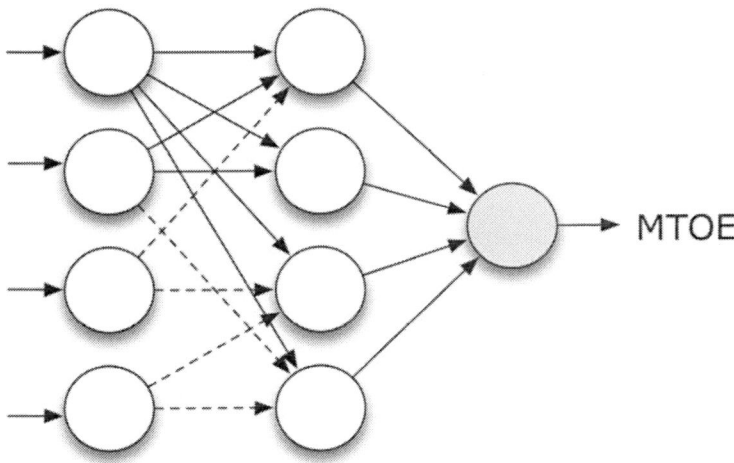

Figure 4. Forecasting 4-4-1 FFANN for energy demand in MTOE.

Figure 4 shows an example of a forecasting network used for estimating the energy demand for a country (Geem & Roper, 2009) where the output in this case is a real-valued signal that represents the energy in million tons oil equivalent (MTOE). Many other forms of such single output unit FFANN are being used for diverse kind of applications such the detection of the amount of rain rate on the ground based on input from a weather radar (Teschl, Randeu & Teschl, 2007). Another example of such networks used as binary classifiers for determining corporate bankruptcy by indicating "No" probability (Nasir, John & Bennett, 2000).

2.3. REPRESENTATION

Neurons are also referred to as processing elements, nodes, or units (Skapura, 1996). The artificial neuron representation shown earlier in Figure 1 is composed of a two-part processing element. The first part sums up the weighted input signals and if this sum is large enough, the neuron is said to fire, i.e. produce output. The second part consists of an activation function for limiting the amplitude of the output of the neuron. The activation function is also known as the neuron transfer function or squashing function since it squashes the permissible amplitude range of the output signal to some finite value (Padhy, 2005). A number of commonly used activation functions are given in Table 1 (Duch & Jankowski, 2000; Debes, Koenig & Gross, 2005).

Table 1. Common neuron activation functions

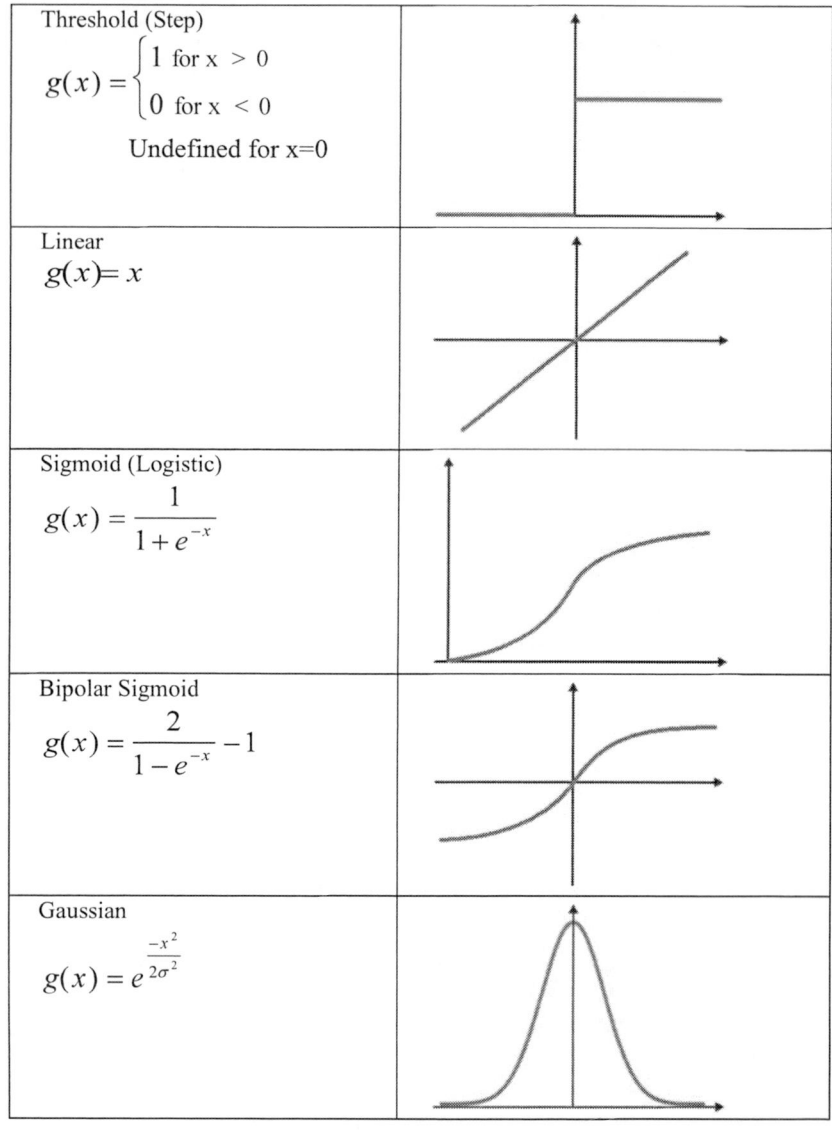

Threshold (Step) $g(x) = \begin{cases} 1 \text{ for } x > 0 \\ 0 \text{ for } x < 0 \end{cases}$ Undefined for x=0	
Linear $g(x) = x$	
Sigmoid (Logistic) $g(x) = \dfrac{1}{1 + e^{-x}}$	
Bipolar Sigmoid $g(x) = \dfrac{2}{1 - e^{-x}} - 1$	
Gaussian $g(x) = e^{\frac{-x^2}{2\sigma^2}}$	

Most FFANNs are based on either sigmoidal or Gaussian transfer functions (Duch & Jankowski, 2000; Moraga, 2007). Sigmoidal functions are commonly used for pattern-classification problems (Liang, 2007) such as the binary sigmoid and the bipolar sigmoid[1] functions. The former normalizes the output amplitude in the interval [0, 1], while the latter in the interval [-1,1] and as shown in Table 1.

The forward-pass calculations for each neuron involve finding the sum of input signals and then applying the activation function. These calculations are expressed in equation (1) and (2) using the bipolar sigmoid as an activation function.

$$y = \sum_{i=1}^{n+1} w_i x_i \tag{1}$$

$$z = F(y) = \frac{2}{1+e^{-y}} - 1 \tag{2}$$

Where:

x_i input value from unit *i* of previous layer (output of that unit)

w_i the weight between this neuron and unit *i* of previous layer (w_{n+1} represents bias)

y sum of the neuron's input signals

n+1 total number of input connections including bias

$F(y)$ neuron transfer function (bipolar sigmoid)

z neuron output

The feed-forward calculations involve finding the network's output by performing the forward-pass calculations for each layer starting from the first input layer and as shown earlier in the FFANN of Figure 2. Such calculations can also be expressed in terms of matrix operations where matrix multiplication is very frequent (Soliman & Mohamed, 2008; Kattan, Abdullah & Salam, 2009a). Figure 5 shows a sample FFANN forward-pass matrix calculation.

---

[1] Closely related to the hyperbolic tangent function.

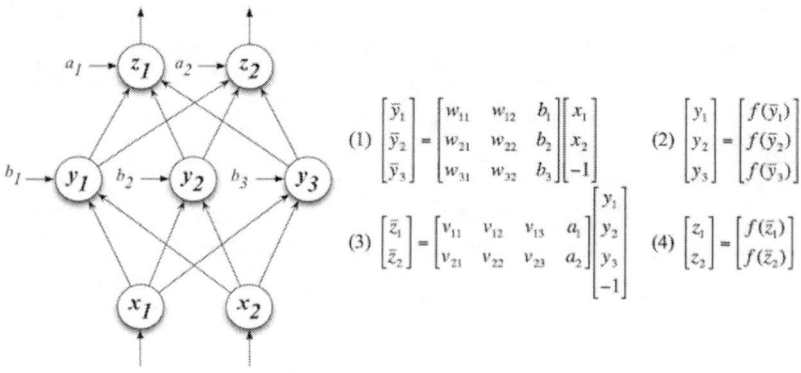

Figure 5. Forward-pass matrix calculations for a sample FFANN.

Chapter 3

FFANN SOFTWARE SIMULATION

In general neural network simulation (implementation) is usually based on different factors including cost, accuracy, processing speed and overall performance. There is always a trade-off between the accuracy of the implementation and the reliability of its performance (Moerland, Fiesler & Beale, 1997). Regardless of the implementation approach such implementation is generally application specific.

It is always preferable to have software-based network architecture in the early stages of application development even if the aim is to eventually have hardware-based implementation. This would facilitate the process of rapidly modifying the network's size and learning method. The design of such hardware is further affected by issues like whether training is conducted off-board or on-board. The latter would affect the size of hardware used and level of parallelism exploited by the hardware. Usually, for such hardware implementations, off-board training is preferred to reduce the size and complexity of the hardware used. In this process a software simulator is still needed to train the network. Once trained, the network's interconnections scheme is then committed to some form of an electronic integrated circuitry making the structure and weights of the network itself fixed (Mathia & Clark, 2002).

It is worth mentioning that the inherent parallelism of large ANNs or those having large training data set, leads to huge amount of computations if they are carried out using a software simulator. Thus for real-time processing tasks, hardware implementation may often be the only viable choice (Bochev, 1993; Jung & Kim, 2007; Duren, Marks II & Reynolds, 2007).

3.1. SEQUENTIAL SOFTWARE SIMULATION

Sequential software simulation on conventional general-purpose computers is considered as the most basic implementation and is usually used as a measure of performance to compare with other approaches of ANNs implementations (Duren, Marks II & Reynolds, 2007; Ferrer *et al.*, 2004). Although nowadays many general-purpose computers are equipped with multi-core processors having a potential similar to that of a parallel computer (Hill & Marty, 2008), the mere availability of such parallel hardware does not guarantee parallel processing (Mathia & Clark, 2002). A sequential software simulation refers to the sequential programming approach taken in simulating the ANN computations.

For such simulation two significant issues must be addressed: memory consumption and overall simulation time (Skapura, 1996). Many factors affect both like the intended precision, which sometimes referred to as the quantization effects (Moerland, Fiesler & Beale, 1997), the number of processing elements as well as the data structures used in general. Due to the many floating-point operations the amount of the needed processing time can grow along with the size of a given ANN and the nature of the computations being conducted. Memory consumption and overall simulation time would have a direct impact in terms of cost.

Using a conventional programming language usually suffices for such computations. However the last decade has witnessed a preference for using an object-oriented programming paradigm for the implementation of such ANN simulators owing to the many merits of this paradigm and the flexibility it offers (El Emam *et al.*, 1991; Albuquerque, 1994; Mehrotra, Venlcatesan & Quaicoe, 1997). A complete example of such Object-Oriented ANN programming paradigm can be found in Rogers (1997) and also in Valentini & Masulli (2002).

3.2. PARALLEL SOFTWARE SIMULATION

The reason for moving to parallel machine should be to solve larger examples of a given problem rather than to solve the same-sized problems more quickly (Freeman & Phillips, 1992). To take advantage of any of the different architectures of parallel computers, two conditions must be met: First, the problem considered must be in principle able to be processed in parallel since parallel processing is not guaranteed by the mere availability of parallel hardware itself. And second, the program code has to reflect the underlying parallel hardware (Seiffert, 2004).

There is no consensus regarding the simulation of ANNs on parallel machines (Kattan, Abdullah & Salam, 2009b). The intrinsic parallel nature of ANN calculations has encouraged researchers to try achieving maximal performance on their favorite, or available, parallel or distributed machines (Chronopoulos & Sarangapani, 2002; Calvert & Guan, 2005).

Based on the general fact that it is only possible to handle independent parts in parallel processes, ANNs with layered topologies, such as FFANNs, seem to be better suited for parallel processing than those having less in a layered structure. This stems from the fact that single-layer calculations are based on the existence or output of a previous layer. The intended parallelization can be achieved either by network partitioning, pattern partitioning, or combination of these two (Chronopoulos & Sarangapani, 2002).

In the first technique, network partitioning, nodes and weights of the ANN are partitioned among different processors. This would cause a parallelization for the computations across the processors. Master-slaves relationship processing model is commonly used here. The master hands over operations to slaves and no slave-to-slave messaging exists (Sykes & Mirkovic, 2005; Calvert & Guan, 2005). This is a form of a centralized approach that aims to lessen the overhead of sending packets between different nodes.

In the second technique, pattern partitioning, the training set is distributed over the processors (slicing) while keeping a complete copy of the whole network in each processor node. The latter technique is particularly suited for FFANNs where the size of the training data is large compared to the size of the network (Howlett & Walters, 1999). The functionality concept of pattern partitioning is described in terms of the patterns used for training the network. In equation (3), a training file F is composed of subsets of training classes. Each subset S_j belonging to a certain class j with a total r. During the training phase the macro-nodes are trained in parallel to convergence with their own modified learning algorithm. If T_c denotes the convergence threshold, then this would be accomplished such that the output of the jth class discriminator is described by (4) and (5) where y is the output and x are the inputs.

$$F = \{S_1 \cup S_2 \cup .. \cup S_r\} \ . \tag{3}$$

$$y_i \geq 1 - T_c \forall x_n \in S_j \, . \tag{4}$$

$$y_i \leq T_c \forall x_m \in S_i (i = 1, ..., r) \ i \neq j \, . \tag{5}$$

Since the total number of processors is limited by the number of training patterns, pattern partitioning is a coarse-grained method that is useful in case of using a training set with a total number of patterns that is much higher than the available processors. The implementation of a neural network on a heterogeneous parallel architecture gives rise to a hard problem. This problem concerns the optimal mapping of the network and of the training patterns among the heterogeneous processors (Siwei, 2000; Milea & Slvasta, 2001; Chronopoulos & Sarangapani, 2002).

The network-partitioning technique on the other hand can be considered more of a fine-grained method. There have been some works that suggest methods used to predict and evaluate the performance of distributed ANN algorithms by analyzing the performance of the comparatively mathematical operations which are used in them. In this case ANN algorithms can be divided into simple components: matrix and vector multiplication, matrix processed through a function and competition (Calvert & Guan, 2005).

If one processor handles each layer then several computations in this case are performed sequentially. This is a sort of coarse-grained concurrency. However, within an FFANN layer, fine grained concurrency can be achieved by further distribution of neuron computations where a computation may be theoretically speeded up to its logical limits over a network of distributed processors (El Emam et al., 1991; Sykes & Mirkovic, 2005).

The programming language used for these parallel software simulation techniques should facilitate code writing to utilize the underlying parallel hardware. For distributed ANN implementation in general, C++ with Message Passing Interface (MPI) is commonly used (Strey, 2004; Pandey, Tapaswi & Srivastava, 2010). Java is also another popular programming language in developing parallel-distributed applications. The success of Java as platform-independent language in developing such applications is not restricted to desktop and server computers but also in developing distributed applications for Java-enabled mobile phones (Kattan et al., 2009a; Kattan et al., 2009b). In addition of being platform-independent two other favorite features make Java a good candidate for such ANN distributed implementations; its vast networking Application Program Interface (API) and Remote Method Invocation (RMI) capability (Goetz et al., 2006; Al-

Jaroodi *et al.*, 2003; Factor, Schuster & Shagin, 2004; Wueng, Yang & Yang, 2004; Koutsogiannakis, Savva & Chang, 2002). The latter feature would enable calling remote methods located on other machines as if the code were local, a feature that will lessen the burden of distributed programming. In addition, the availability of integrated development environments written in Java would provide a common and consistent development platform across a wide range of systems (Kattan, Abdullah & Salam, 2006).

Chapter 4

FFANN TRAINING CONCEPT

The supervised training of FFANNs involves a repetitive process of presenting a training data set to the network's input and determining the error between the actual network's output and the intended target output. In mathematical formalism training refers to the process by which the FFANN weight coefficients are adjusted in such a way, that the calculated and desired outputs are as close as possible (Svozil, Kvasnicka & Pospichal, 1997). Such process is referred to as supervised training.

The supervised training process is shown in Figure 6. The individual neuron weights are then adjusted to minimize such error and give the FFANN its generalization ability. Several forms of error calculations can be considered and these are discussed in section 4.2. A learning or training algorithm is responsible for adjusting the FFANN weights coefficient using some form of error calculations as a measure (Fausett, 1994; Padhy, 2005).

In some forms of learning the weight adjustment process could be postponed till after presenting all training patterns (Kattan, Abdullah & Salam, 2009a). This iterative process continues until some criteria are satisfied, which is known as the termination conditions. This usually happens based on some measure, calculated or estimated, indicating that the current achieved solution is presumably good enough to stop training (Padhy, 2005).

There are basically two major FFANN supervised training paradigms, the classical trajectory-driven paradigm and the evolutionary-based stochastic paradigm. These are introduced in chapter 5 and chapter 6 respectively.

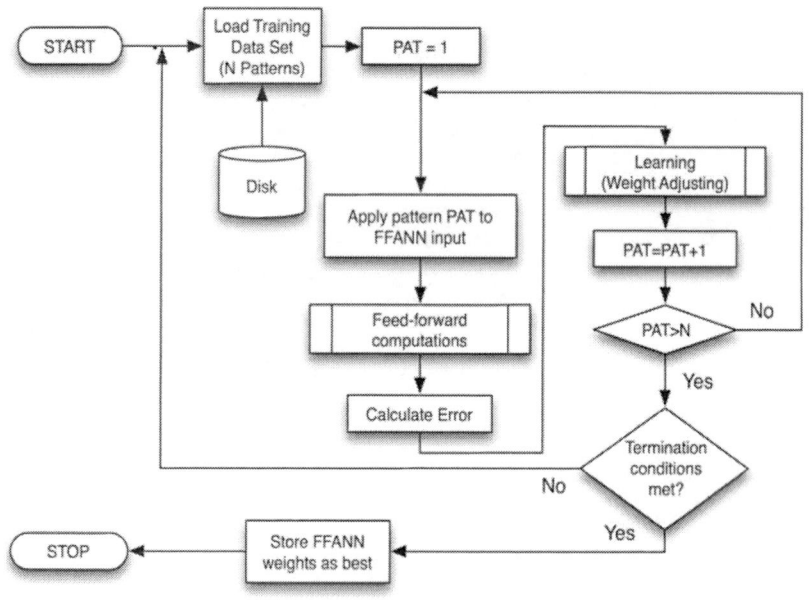

Figure 6. FFANN supervised training concept.

4.1. TRAINING DATA PREPARATIONS

Supervised training involves preparing a set of training vectors, or patterns, such that each of these vectors is associated with a target output vector. This is in contrast to other forms of unsupervised ANN learning where the data set lacks a target output and it's the role of the network to cluster the data based on similarities (Hassoun, 1995).

A common practice is to split the problem's data set to use 70% - 80% of the patterns as training set and the rest for post training out-of-sample testing set (Delgado, Pegalajar & Cuellar, 2006; Wei, 2007). The training set and testing set are made to include equal percentages of each class, i.e. equal percentages of each pattern type.

Another common practice is to split the problem's data into three sets, use the largest for training, one for out-of-sample testing and one for validation. The latter is used during training to validate the recognition ability of the network after the weight adjustment process in order to give judgment on its generalization ability (Hassoun, 1995).

However, if the problem's data set is relatively small then such data set segmentation will make the size of the training data set insufficient to train the network. Section 4.3 will address the advantage of such data set segmentation technique in terms of determining the termination condition.

4.2. ERROR CALCULATIONS

There are different ways to perform the error calculations in the supervised training technique depending primarily on the nature of application the network was designed for. It is usually a goal of researcher to find suitable error calculation within a short training time that is appropriate for the network's application. A summary of the common error calculation formulas that are used for pattern-classification problems is given in Table 2 and discussed below.

Apart from the last two formulas, PCCE and CEP, all of these error calculation formals are based on calculating the squared difference between the network's output and the intended target output namely $(t_i - z_i)^2$. The last two error formulas report the network's classification ability in percentage format.

The sum of square errors (SSE) is the most popular error function (Dorsey, Johnson & Mayer, 1994; Siddique & Tokhi, 2001; Fish *et al.*, 2004). The least square error (LSE) is simply SSE multiplied by one half which has no impact on the final solution is also commonly used (Geem, Kim & Loganathan, 2002; Wei, 2007). MSE is also commonly used as an error formula (Zhang & Wu, 2008; Yu, Wang & Xi, 2008).

It is often useful to use the root-mean-square error (RMSE) and the normalized RMSE (NRMSE) instead of SSE and LSE (Hassoun, 1995; Rocha, Cortez & Neves, 2007) since as the number of training patterns P increases the value of SSE or LSE also increases. For the latter, NRMSE, the value is limited to the range of [0,1] where a smallest value of zero indicates that the network can predict the training set exactly.

The last two formulas, namely the percentage of correctly classified examples (PCCE) and the classification error percentage (CEP), can be used to complement SSE, LSE and MSE raw error values since both reports in a high-level manner the quality of the trained network (Alba & Chicano, 2004).

Table 2. Summary of common error calculation formulas

Sum of Square Errors (**SSE**):	$$SSE = \sum_{p=1}^{P}\sum_{i=1}^{S}(t_i^p - z_i^p)^2$$
Least Square Error (**LSE**)	$$LSE = \frac{1}{2}\sum_{p=1}^{P}\sum_{i=1}^{S}(t_i^p - z_i^p)^2$$
Mean Square Error (**MSE**)	$$MSE = \frac{1}{P \cdot S}\sum_{p=1}^{P}\sum_{i=1}^{S}(t_i^p - z_i^p)^2$$
Root-Mean-Square Error (**RMSE**)	$$RMSE = \sqrt{\frac{1}{P \cdot S}\sum_{p=1}^{P}\sum_{i=1}^{S}(t_i^p - z_i^p)^2}$$
Normalized RMSE (**NRMSE**)	$$NRMSE = \frac{RMSE}{(\sum_{p=1}^{P}\sum_{i=1}^{S}t_i^p)/P} \times 100\%$$
Squared Error Percentage (**SEP**)	$$SEP = 100 \cdot \frac{z_{max} - z_{min}}{P \cdot S}\sum_{p=1}^{P}\sum_{i=1}^{S}(t_i^p - z_i^p)^2$$
Percentage of Correctly Classified Examples (**PCCE**)	$$\Phi(k) = \begin{cases} 1 & \text{if } T_k = Z_k \\ 0 & \text{Otherwise} \end{cases}$$ $$PCCE = \sum_{k=1}^{P}\Phi(k)/P \times 100\%$$
Classification Error Percentage (**CEP**)	$$CEP = \frac{E_P}{P} \cdot 100\%$$

Where
- P   total number of training patterns
- S   total number of output units (classes)
- t   target output (unit)
- z   actual neuron output (unit)
- $\Phi(k)$ threshold output for pattern k
- T   target output vector
- Z   network output vector
- E_p total number of incorrectly recognized training patterns

4.3. TERMINATION CONDITIONS

Based on the use of the error calculation formulas presented in the previous section, many learning algorithms would stop the training process once the difference between the error calculated in the current learning cycle and that of the previous is less than a certain small error value acceptable for the application (Hassoun, 1995; Padhy, 2005). However, it was found that it is not necessarily advantageous to continue training until this error actually reaches a minimum (Fausett, 1994). Training the network more than necessary would cause it to eventually lose its generalization ability to recognize out-of-sample patterns, a condition known as overtraining or overfitting (Liu, Starzyk & Zhu, 2008). Underfitting on the other hand occurs when training is terminated prematurely or the used network structure is unable to learn well from the training data set used (Lawrence & Giles, 2000; Palmes & Usui, 2005).

Although other factors might cause the overfitting and the underfitting problems such as the size of the network, size of the training set and the amount of weight changes (Palmes & Usui, 2005) stopping the training process must take into consideration these factors. The main motivation behind using a training or learning algorithm is to eventually achieve a balance between the correct response of the network to the training patterns and good response to new input patterns. Put in another way a balance between memorization and generalization (Fausett, 1994).

One of the methods suggested to elevate these problems is to use two sets of data during training, a training set and a validation set as presented earlier in section 4.1. The validation set is used at certain intervals during training after the learning process in order to compute the error for this set. As long as this error keeps decreasing training continues. Once this error starts to increase, then it's an indication that the network is starting to memorize the training patterns too specifically such that it will gradually lose its ability to generalize. The error for the training set however would continue to decrease. Many other techniques have been suggested such as pre-processing the training data in a certain way by filtering certain features (Rosin & Fierens, 1995) or evaluating a certain criterion in order to do what is known as "early stopping". Early stopping aims to stop the training process at the point that is believed that the network would starts to lose its generalization ability (Caruana, Lawrence & Giles, 2000; Iyer & Rhinehart, 2000; Liu, Starzyk & Zhu, 2008).

Chapter 5

TRAJECTORY-DRIVEN TRAINING PARADIGM

Trajectory-driven FFANN supervised training methods dates back to more than two decades ago. The mathematical calculations used within these methods are basically a form of trajectory calculations including vector derivatives from which the term trajectory-driven is taken.

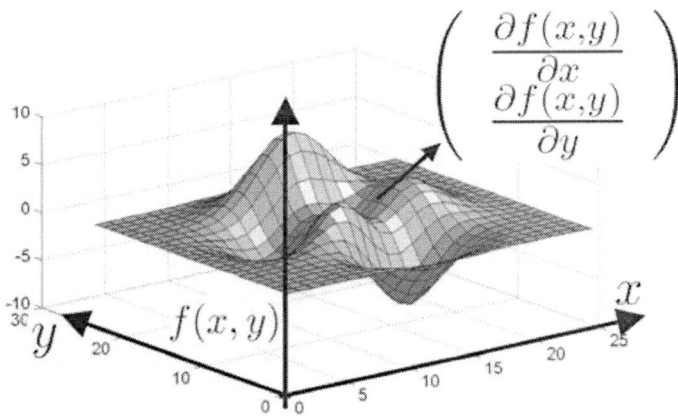

Figure 7. The gradient-descent technique in a 3-dimensional error surface.

A necessity in all trajectory-driven methods is for the neuron activation function to be differentiable (Fausett, 1994). The main concept behind all of these methods is the utilization of the calculation of the mathematical gradient descent. The gradient descent of the current error surface is calculated in order to minimize total error on the patterns in the training set as shown earlier in Figure 6. The main difference between these methods is how the gradient descent information is utilized to compute the weight update amounts after each training epoch(s).

The concept is illustrated in Figure 7 using a simplified 3-dimensional error surface where in reality such surface is multi-dimensional. The gradient is used to locate minima points and the information is used to adjust the network weights accordingly in order to minimize the output error. All of these methods have the common disadvantage of their tendency to converge to a local minimum near its starting point (Liang, 2007). FFANN tend to generate complex error surfaces with multiple local minima and trajectory-driven methods possess the possibility of being trapped in local solution that is not global (Gupta & Sexton, 1999).

In spite of this disadvantage many trajectory-driven methods have been used successfully for the supervised training of ANNs. The most commonly used methods that can be found in the literature include Backpropagation (BP), Conjugate Gradient (CG), Quasi-Newton's (QN), and the Levenberg-Marquardt (LM) algorithm (Liang, 2007).

A detailed discussion of each of these trajectory-driven methods is beyond the scope of this work. However BP, being a more popular supervised learning method in comparison to others (Chronopoulos & Sarangapani, 2002), will be covered with some details in the next section. The subsequent section will briefly give the basics for the rest of these methods and highlights some of their differences and advantages.

5.1. BACKPROPAGATION TRAINING

One of the most popular supervised training methods for FFANNs is the BP learning algorithm (Chronopoulos & Sarangapani, 2002; Kathirvalavakumar & Thangavel, 2006; Geem & Roper, 2009). The BP algorithm adjusts the weights in the steepest descent direction, which is simply the negative of the gradient.

However BP, as a trajectory-driven method, is generally considered to be inefficient in searching for global minimum of the search space (Kim, Kim & Chung, 2005). The BP training process is associated with two major problems; slow convergence for complex problems and local minima entrapment (Kathirvalavakumar & Thangavel, 2006; Nasr & Chtourou, 2006).

Different techniques have been proposed to cure these problems to a certain extent including techniques such as simulated annealing and dynamic tunneling (Kathirvalavakumar & Thangavel, 2006). The use of some special weight initialization techniques such as the Nguyen-Widrow method would lessen the possibility of converging to a local minimum (Fausett, 1994; Guijarro-Berdinas *et al.*, 2006; Škutova, 2008). BP could also use a momentum constant in it's learning rule, where such technique accelerates the training process in flat regions of the error surface and prevents fluctuations in the weights (Geem & Roper, 2009). A full coverage of the BP algorithm can be found in (Fausett, 1994) and (Padhy, 2005).

5.2. OTHER COMMON TRAJECTORY-DRIVEN TRAINING METHODS

When using the BP training method, weights are adjusted in the direction that is negative of the gradient, which is the steepest descent direction. In the CG training method a search is conducted along conjugate directions, which generally produces faster convergence than steepest descent directions (Hagan, Demuth & Beale, 1996).

An alternative to the CG method is the Newton's method. This method involves second derivatives for the Hessian matrix of the performance index (error) at the current values of the weights. The method converges faster than CG but calculating the Hessian matrix would be computationally expensive. The QN method is based on Newton's method but does not require the calculation of the second derivatives. Instead an approximate Hessian matrix is updated at each training iteration as a function of the gradient (Dennis & Schnabel, 1983).

LM is similar to the QN method in that it doesn't require the computation of the Hessain matrix second derivatives and uses another form of approximation of this matrix (Hagan & Menhaj, 1994).

A more recent review of the trajectory-driven methods presented here can be found in (Abraham, 2004) with comparisons to the evolutionary-based paradigm presented next. It is worth mentioning that improved versions of these methods and various types of applications that are based on them are continually being introduced in the literature (Bascil & Temurtas, 2009; Kostopoulos & Grapsa, 2009; Cetişli & Barkana, 2010; Jayalakshmi & Santhakumaran, 2010).

Chapter 6

EVOLUTIONARY-BASED TRAINING PARADIGM

Evolutionary-based supervised training methods offer an alternative to trajectory-driven methods. These are stochastic global optimization (SGO) techniques that are the result of combining an evolutionary optimization algorithm (EA) with the ANN learning process (Gao, 2008). Evolutionary algorithms are usually inspired from biological or physical processes such as Genetic Algorithms (GA) (Kim, Kim & Chung, 2005), Ant Colony Optimization (ACO) (Wei, 2007), Improved Bacterial Chemo-taxis Optimization (IBCO) (Zhang & Wu, 2008), and Particle Swarm Optimization (PSO) (Yu, Wang & Xi, 2008). The concept behind such EAs is the fitness of a population as shown in the flowchart of Figure 8. Many of these evolutionary training techniques have reported improvements in computation precision and efficiency in comparison with trajectory-driven methods such as BP. However, it is worth mentioning that many of these reported improvements were based on implementations using the classical XOR problem (Alba & Chicano, 2004; Kim, Kim & Chung, 2005; Wei, 2007; Zhang & Wu, 2008). This problem, in addition of being a very small scale FFANN implementation, is also a special case. It was proven that the XOR problem has no local minima (Hamey, 1998). Considering multiple problems of larger data sets would solidify such type of comparisons (Abraham, 2004; Rocha, Cortez & Neves, 2007).

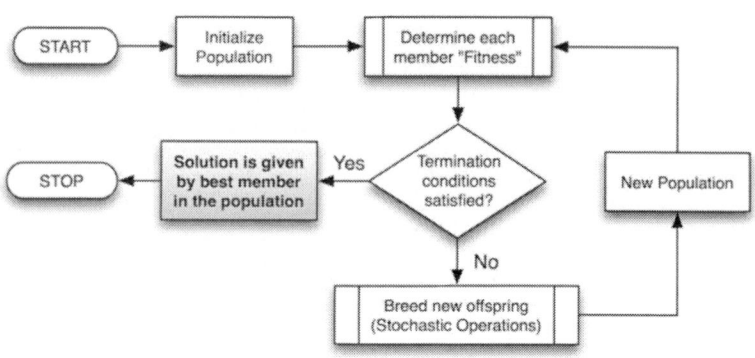

Figure 8. Evolutionary algorithm concept.

A population is composed of a set of entities, referred to as members, representing features of individuals of the current generation population. Environmental pressure causes natural selection, which in turn causes a rise in the fitness of that population. An evaluation function, commonly referred to as fitness function, represents a heuristic estimation of solution quality and the variation and selection operators drive the search process. Recombination is mostly used in EAs to mix information of more candidate solutions to form new ones; a process for breeding new offspring (Eiben & Smith, 2008). Such evolutionary methods are expected to avoid local minima frequently by promoting exploration of the search space. Their explorative search features differ from those of BP in that they are not trajectory-driven, but population driven. Using such SGO methods for neural network training, many if not all problems associated with BP can be overcome (Gupta & Sexton, 1999).

Merging the EA concept, illustrated in Figure 8, with that of the FFANN supervised learning process, given earlier in Figure 6, results in an evolutionary-based learning method. The EA solution in this case represents the final trained network in terms of values for its different parameters such as weight values, structure or leaning parameters (Abraham, 2004). The merits of such evolutionary-based training methods is that they overcome the local-minima entrapment problem of the trajectory-driven methods and they can be applied where gradient information is either not available, costly to obtain or the neuron activation function is non-differentiable (Siddique & Tokhi, 2001).

There are three basic concerns that an evolutionary-based training method must address. These are

- The FFANN data representation.
- The fitness function.
- The termination conditions.

Data representation for FFANN is a scheme to represent the network weights (including biases) as well as the network's parameters and structure. The fitness function is used to decide how good the new offspring solution is and finally the termination condition would decide when training should stop.

The most common evolutionary-based FFANN supervised training methods includes GA, ACO and PSO based methods. GA is very popular and is more ubiquitous than the latter two in terms of its application. GA-based supervised training will be covered with more detailed within the next section. The subsequent section will cover some works on the latter methods, namely ACO and PSO evolutionary-based training methods.

6.1. GENETIC-ALGORITHM BASED TRAINING METHODS

The field of genetic algorithms was created by Holland (1975) and was an early land mark. GA uses a population of individuals representing tentative solution vectors. The canonical algorithm would apply stochastic operators on these individuals such as selection, crossover and mutation to generate new offspring. A fitness function is used as a measure to the quality of each solution which is reflected in its selection process (Alba & Chicano, 2004). There are many variations of this algorithm but regardless of these variations GA has been successfully used as a supervised learning algorithm. Though the algorithm cannot guarantee convergence to the global minimum, it can produce quite acceptable or near optimal solutions (Montana, 1995; Padhy, 2005). The application of GA to the supervised training of FFANN will be addressed in terms of the three basic concerns outlined in the previous section, namely representation, fitness function and termination.

In the most basic form of GA-based learning the problem of FFANN is formulated as:

$$\text{Maximize } f(s), \text{ Subject to } s \in \Omega = \{0,1\}^n \tag{6}$$

Where $f : \Omega \rightarrow R$ is the fitness function, and the n-dimensional binary vectors in Ω are called strings representing groups of chromosomes. These strings could represent the network weight values, learning parameters, topology, and type of activation functions or a mixture out of these (Yao, 1993; Siddique & Tokhi, 2001; Huang *et al.*, 2009). Typically, the maximization of f would in this case result in a form of reduction in the network output error, which is the bases behind this learning method (Hassoun, 1995).

6.1.1. Representation

Classical representation of the population strings is usually binary-coded such that the parameters in this string are encoded from the real-valued space into the binary space (Hassoun, 1995). The former space is known as phenotype space while the latter is known as genotype space (Eiben & Smith, 2008). Obtaining the solutions would involve a reverse decoding process where the parameter **n** in equation (6) would determine the precision of the obtained results. It has been shown that such binary representation is neither necessary nor beneficial and it limits the effectiveness of the GA (Gupta & Sexton, 1999). Using too few bits will take extremely long time or even cause the training convergence to fail. On the other hand too many bits will take more processing time prolonging the evolution process to the point that it becomes impractical. Real-coded weight representation was used in GA to train neural networks where such technique proved to be more efficient in comparison to the binary-coded one (Siddique & Tokhi, 2001; Fish *et al.*, 2004). In spite of this deficiency, the binary-coded approach is still being used in some recent works to search for the optimal network parameters like number of hidden units, training parameters, etc. excluding weight values (Ferentinos, 2005; Huang *et al.*, 2009).

In GA-based training with real-coded representation, each member of the population, namely a vector, represents a whole set of weights for the FFANN assuming a fixed architecture network. For such a representation, the works of Montana & Davis (1989) and that of Montana (1995) are ones of the first works that can be tracked on the application of GA for the training of FFANN with fixed architecture. Using experimentation data taken from an underwater sonar system they tested the proposed GA-based training algorithm for the detection of various signals and compared the results to those of BP. The proposed algorithm comprises of a representation, different type of genetic operators, evaluation function and an initialization procedure. The population members (strings) consist of real-coded lists formed out of weights and biases starting from the output layer down to the input layer. Each weight value is atomic and different operators operate on such values.

A minor variation to the former representation approach was used in the GANNT algorithm (Genetic Adaptive Neural Network Training) originally introduced by Dorsey et. al. (1994) and adopted in many GA-based FFANN training applications (Sexton, Dorsey & Jhonson, 1998; Sexton & Dorsey, 2000; Fish *et al.*, 2004; Sexton, Dorsey & Sikander, 2004; Kattan, Abdullah & Salam, 2010). In this technique only the order in which weights are listed in differs. Instead of starting from the output layer, the weight vector is formed by starting from the input layer and as shown in Figure 9.

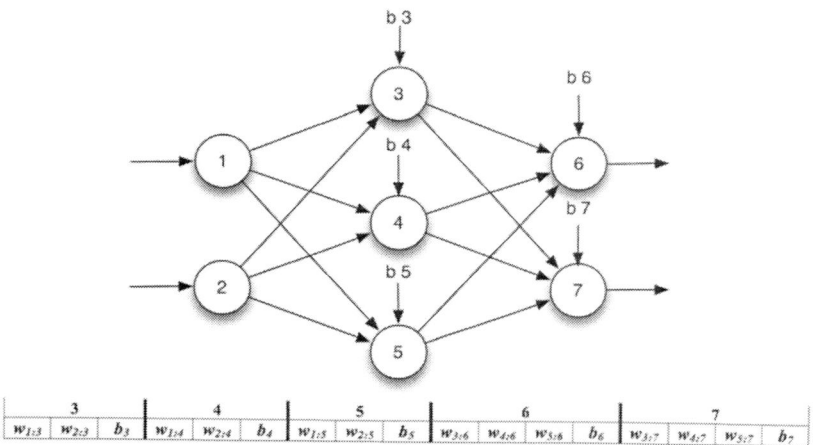

Figure 9. Sample real-coded GA string representation of FFANN.

Another form of string representation is based on the adjacency matrix. The adjacency matrix, also known as the connectivity matrix, introduced a compact way to represent the connections and weight values in any ANN by means of a matrix (Fiesler & Fulcher, 1994). For FFANNs this is a 2-dimensional array where each element represents a connection and its associated weight. Zero valued elements would indicate no connection. Due to the topology of FFANNs the shape of this matrix is an upper or lower diagonal matrix with bias weight values forming the diagonal of this matrix and as shown in Figure 10 (Kim, Kim & Chung, 2005). In this case the matrix is treated as a chromosome and operators such as crossover would be conducted in either row-wise or column-wise fashion while preserving the structure of the network (Siddique & Tokhi, 2001).

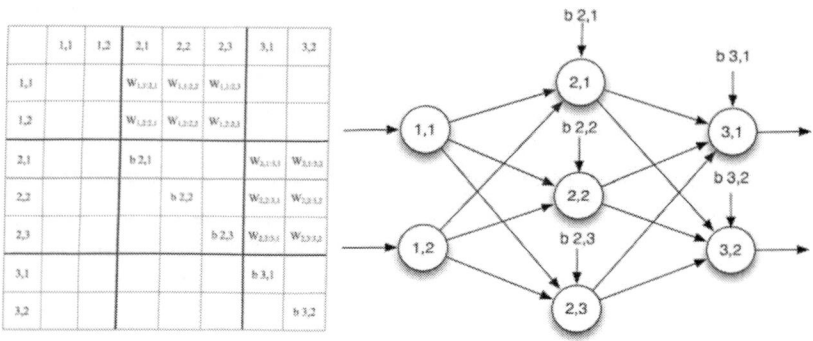

Figure 10. Sample adjacency matrix representation of FFANN.

6.1.2. Fitness Function

Deciding if new breed of weights are better or worst must be based on a measure represented by the fitness function. For fixed architecture FFANN several types of fitness functions have been used for GA-based training methods. In these methods, the algorithm main goal is to search for the optimal weight values. The fitness function in most of these methods would include a basic or a modified version of the error formulas presented earlier in Table 2. Since the problem in GA-based methods are viewed as maximization problems, the negative or the inverse of the aforementioned fitness functions is commonly used.

The most common fitness functions are those that are based on the SSE or MSE formula (Montana & Davis, 1989; Dorsey, Johnson & Mayer, 1994; Montana, 1995; Sexton & Dorsey, 2000; Siddique & Tokhi, 2001; Kim, Kim & Chung, 2005; Ferentinos, 2005), the RMSE formula (Sexton, Dorsey & Jhonson, 1998; Gupta & Sexton, 1999; Sexton, Dorsey & Sikander, 2004), the SEP and CEP formulas (Sexton & Dorsey, 2000; Alba & Chicano, 2004).

6.1.3. Termination Conditions

In addition to the validation set termination method presented earlier, other different ways to stop the learning process within a GA-based method exist. The common standard way for GA-based method is simply based on a pre-specified maximum generation count (Montana & Davis, 1989; Gupta &

Sexton, 1999; Ferentinos, 2005). Others would use some sort of error difference check between the best fitness obtained in the current generation and that of the previous one (Dorsey, Johnson & Mayer, 1994; Fish *et al.*, 2004). Another a bit more computationally expensive test is the percentage of the domination of a certain population member where comparisons are made between the current population members to find matching ones (Hassoun, 1995). The latter is more suited for binary-coded representations though such termination test could be also used with real-coded representation but based on comparisons of the fitness values only (Kattan, Abdullah & Salam, 2010).

6.2. OTHER COMMON EVOLUTIONARY-BASED TRAINING METHODS

Another innovative computational and behavioral metaphor for solving distributed problems is the Swarm Intelligence (SI). SI takes its inspiration from the behavior of social insects and the swarming, flocking, herding and phenomena of vertebrates (Conforth & Meng, 2008). Two well-known and successful bio-inspired SI computational paradigms are the ACO and the PSO (Padhy, 2005). These have been used as a type of evolutionary-based supervised FFANN training methods. They are being used to either evolve the network's weight values, the network's structure (topology & parameters) or both. Conceptually, these methods are iterative methods that follow the same trend used in GA-based methods in terms of having a representation, fitness function, and a termination condition (Blum & Socha, 2005; Mullen *et al.*, 2009). In the next following sections the concept behind each is outlined and some FFANN training applications that are based on these are introduced.

6.2.1. Ant Colony Optimization Based Training Methods

ACO was originally invented by Dorigo et. al. (1996) as a new optimization technique. ACO is based on the ants' foraging behavior that has a form of indirect communication between the ants. Such communication is established by means of chemical pheromone trails. The higher density of this pheromone enables ants to find the short paths between their nest and food sources. This is the main characteristic of real ant colonies that is being exploited in ACO algorithms in order to solve optimization problems (Blum, 2005). ACO exhibits many similarities to evolutionary computing techniques where both employ a population of individuals to incrementally breed better solutions to a given problem based on the solutions of previous populations (Mullen *et al.*, 2009).

Blum and Socha (2005) have used ACO for the training of a fixed architecture FFANN pattern-classifier for a set of classification problems from the medical field using real-valued vector representation for the network's weights. They indicated that the proposed ACO algorithm utilizes a continuous probability density function as opposed to other ACO techniques where the probability distribution is discrete. All solutions in the population are ranked according to their quality measured by their SEP value (see Table 2) with the best having rank 1. They indicated that using ranks instead of the actual fitness function values would make the algorithm insensitive to the scaling of the fitness function. Termination would occur upon reaching a maximum iteration number. The performance of the proposed ACO-based method was measured against other training methods such as BP, LM and GA as well as hybrid versions of their proposed ACO-based training. The hybrid versions would execute a single iteration of a local search method such as BP before solutions are to be evaluated by ACO. Results have indicated that the proposed approach is comparable to these trajectory-driven methods and the hybrid ACO version outperformed the standard ACO.

Another ACO-based learning method is proposed by Wei (2007) that evolves both the network's weights as well as the number of the hidden layer units. Population members utilize a matrix weight representation and compute the fitness values based on an inverse derived from LSE (see Table 2). Learning would terminate either on a maximum iteration count or a minimum error value for the best member; a technique that is used in other ACO-based training methods (Shi & Li, 2009). Wei (2007) reported that his proposed ACO training method has higher precision and efficiency in comparison with BP. However such findings were based on the XOR problem implementation with its known shortcomings discussed earlier.

6.2.2. Particle Swarm Optimization
Based Training Methods

PSO was proposed by Eberhat and Kennedy (1995) inspired by social behavior of bird flocking or fish schooling. PSO is population-driven method where each member is known as "particle" representing a bird or a fish. Each particle in this case is a candidate solution that is initialized with random position and search velocity. The population in this case represents the swarm and each of the particles flies through the problem's space and keeps track of its position and fitness. The fitness is the best solution achieved, or the swarm leader, and the position and velocity are adjusted by its fitness to the environment (Zhou *et al.*, 2006).

PSO has been used for the training of FFANN to either learn the weight values, the network structure or both. Greethanjali et. al. (2008) designed a pattern-classifier FFANN to differentiate the different operating conditions of power transformers. The FFANN weights, represented by particles, evolved using a PSO-based method. At each iteration each particle is updated by following two best values; the best fitness achieved so far and the best value obtained so far by any particle in the population, which is tracked by the algorithm. The velocity and position of each particle is adjusted such that the optimal value of weights is found to meet a pre-specified MSE fitness. The problem used a population of 20 particles but it was indicated that for most problems 10 particles is large enough to get good results. The maximum number of specified iterations and a minimum error requirement usually determines termination. Results where compared to those obtained by BP and the proposed PSO-based training reported to achieve higher accuracy in less overall training time.

Another similar application is proposed by Zhou et. al. (2006) to design a forecasting FFANN to detect the diameter error compensation in a boring machine[1]. PSO-based training was also used to evolve the FFANN weights using the fitness measure of SSE in a population of 30 particles. Training would also halt based on a maximum iteration number and minimum error requirement. Junyou (2007) also designed a forecasting FFANN for Singapore stock market index using a similar construct but using RMSE instead of SSE. Both of the two former PSO-based implementations reported superiority over BP.

Kiranyaz et. al. (2009) used PSO not to evolve the FFANN weights but the design and structure. Particles are to reflect the network configuration with MSE as a fitness funciton and conventional BP to test the generalization ability of the network by running it several times over a set of benchmarking problems. It was indicated that using this BP approach does not guarantee

---

[1] A boring machine is a device for producing smooth and accurate holes in a workpiece by enlarging existing holes with a bore, which may bear a single cutting tip of steel, cemented carbide, or diamond or may be a small grinding wheel.

that the soltion will converge to the global optimal; however the idea is that under equal training conditions, the "trend" of best performances achievable can be obtained with every network configuration. Reported results indicated that networks structures obtained are optimum or near-optimum in terms of their generalization ability.

Yu et. al. (2008) proposed ESPnet; an improved version of PSO and discrete PSO (DPSO) for the joint optimization of FFANN weights and structure. Both are evolved simultaneously such that the structure is evolved by DPSO, while the connections weights by PSO. Each member in the population is represented by a hierarchy structure, in which each consists of a multilevel dimension. Data representation used a form of connectivity matrices such that a bit-matrix is used for connectivity and another real-matrix for weight values. The proposed technique obtained very competitive results in comparison with some other algorithms but at the cost of additional computation time needed to perform the additional DPSO operations. However, they have indicated that for many applications the achieved generalization is more important than the overall training time.

Chapter 7

FFANN SIMULATION UTILIZING GRAPHIC-PROCESSING UNITS

Recently, the demand of the gaming and film-making industries for accelerated rendering of 3D graphic animations, have driven graphic hardware companies to develop high-performance, parallel and real-time graphic-processing units (GPUs) to provide smooth and vivid graphics (Ho, Lam & Leung, 2008). Such hardware became cheap commodity on personal computer systems with a computation power that is surpassing that of general processors in terms of floating point computation and memory bandwidth. The price-to-performance ratio of such graphic processors in addition to their programmability & arithmetic precision has attracted attention of many within the high-performance computing community (McCormick *et al.*, 2008). For general purpose computing, the GPU architecture lends itself well to applications where the same calculations are repeatedly performed on large blocks of data (Meuth & Wunsch II, 2007).

General purpose GPU (GPGPU) is now a well established field in the literature that uses such devices for diverse scientific and engineering applications. Usually, researchers in the GPGPU arena include people from fields like science and physical computation, particle simulation, bioinformatics and so on (Huang *et al.*, 2008; Che *et al.*, 2008). Such GPUs can be thought of as highly parallel single instruction multiple data (SIMD) type of processors (Atanasov, 2005; Ho, Lam & Leung, 2008). However, the units of the GPU do not include efficient branching hardware. Therefore algorithms with branching operations are difficult to implement effectively. In addition the GPU data transfer bus is usually inefficient for small data transfers. Data in this case must be operated in batches to achieve a reasonable speedup. Many of these issues and limitations have been overcome by the design of creative algorithms and implementations to target systems (Meuth & Wunsch II, 2007).

7.1. GPU PROGRAMMING PARADIGMS

For an algorithm to execute efficiently on a GPU, it must be cast into a data-parallel form with many thousands of independent threads running in an SIMD fashion (Anderson, Lorenz & Travesset, 2008). Nowadays GPUs contain a large number of general purpose processors, in sharp contrast to previous generation designs, where special-purpose hardware units were commonly used. In spite of that, GPU programming is still substantially more difficult and requires more effort than developing multithreaded applications suitable for execution on multi-core CPUs (Marziale, Richard III & Roussev, 2007).

The first programming paradigm is a graphic-centric technique inherited from the previous generation of GPUs. Performing non-graphical calculations required techniques that recast data as textures or geometric primitives and expressed the calculations in terms of available graphical operations (Marziale, Richard III & Roussev, 2007). Developers must deal with the mapping of the computation into graphic primitives and operations (Meuth & Wunsch II, 2007). Such programming trend is of a cumbersome nature where various limitations are imposed (Anderson, Lorenz & Travesset, 2008). Though such development process would involve writing low-level code, many APIs and libraries exist such as OpenGL or DirectX that can facilitate this process (Atanasov, 2005; Meuth & Wunsch II, 2007). However, the programming style is still similar to assembly and requires a deep understanding of such architectures.

The second GPU programming paradigm is owed to the advent of new line of GPU hardware. Such hardware have allowed for a more flexible and general-purpose approach due to their new architectures. They contain a large number of general-purpose processors, also known as stream processors, causing them to excel at executing massively threaded algorithms (Marziale, Richard III & Roussev, 2007). Many C-style like GPU programming languages have emerged such as Brook and RapidMind to provide data abstraction and useful functions reducing the learning curve of these devices (Meuth & Wunsch II, 2007). nVidia's CUDA is one of the latest more successful C-style programming tools that have facilitated this process further by providing a thread-based programming model for graphic hardware (Meuth & Wunsch II, 2007; Jang, Park & Jung, 2008; Dolan &

DeSouza, 2009). Due to the extremely multithreaded nature of the GPU, programming the GPU using such a language is very different from general purpose programming on the CPU.

Che et. al. (2008) have compared the performance of CPU and GPU implementations of six naturally data-parallel applications using OpenMP (Open Multi-Processing) for multi-core CPU programming versus CUDA. The latter have showed a great potential for general purpose computing whereby impressive speedups where obtained. They have highlighted that CUDA is far easier than the traditional graphic-centric technique. A more recent C-Style language is OpenCL originally developed by Apple. OpenCL is a parallel computing framework for programming multi-core systems including both GPUs and other multi-core CPUs (Tsuchiyama *et al.*, 2010).

7.2. ANN GPU-BASED SIMULATION TECHNIQUES

Although the simulation of an ANN can be accomplished using software, many potential applications require real-time processing utilizing fully parallel and specially designed hardware (Duren, Marks II & Reynolds, 2007; Jung & Kim, 2007). Generally the basic trend in simulating ANNs on GPUs is to reduce the neural network computations into a series of matrix operations based on the approach presented earlier in section 2.3. Thus they are easily parallelized, as the GPU is highly optimized to perform these kinds of operations (Meuth & Wunsch II, 2007). Learning is still carried out using the techniques discussed previously.

Oh & Jung (2004) have implemented a FFANN utilizing a GPU. They indicated that the main issue in using FFANNs for image processing and pattern recognition applications is the computational complexity. The parallelism of the GPU has been fully utilized by accumulating a lot of input feature vectors and weight vectors, then converting the many inner-product operations into one matrix operation. The graphic-centric programming paradigm, mentioned in the previous section, was used for implementation. It is important to indicate that this paradigm was the only one available on the graphic hardware of the time.

Jang et. al. (2008) have indicated that for GPU-based applications a job would needs much cooperation between the CPU and the GPU. This sort of hardware arrangement where the GPU is much faster than CPU in term of performing its operations would usually create a gap in which the GPU would wait for data to be completed and processed by the CPU. They have implemented a multi-threaded FFANN application for text detection in pages. The FFANN is to classify the pixels of input image and all neural operations are represented by matrices inner product and carried out on the GPU utilizing CUDA. The multi-core CPU generates the data as soon as possible utilizing OpenMP to help concurrently process multiple data. The efficiency of the proposed method is accomplished by the parallel use of the CPU and GPU. The reported text detection was 20 times faster than the CPU alone implementation and 5 times faster than GPU alone implementation.

The speedup in computations offered by GPUs and the accessibility to the programming features of such hardware would render the simulation of larger ANN achievable on commodity computers.

Chapter 8

CONCLUSION

ANNs are developed as generalization of mathematical models of human neural biology. The degree in which a network models a certain biological system varies. In general, ANNs have the main advantage of being able to use some priori unknown information hidden in data where they can realize an arbitrary mapping between one vector space into another vector space. FFANNs are a special class of ANNs that is characterized by a topology of fully connected layers with no closed paths or lateral connections. This class of networks has achieved increased popularity among engineers, scientists as well as other professionals in the field of pattern-recognition and forecasting applications.

ANNs simulation is based on different factors including cost, accuracy, processing speed and overall performance. Sequential simulation on conventional general-purpose computers is considered as the most basic and usually used as measure of performance to compare to other approaches. Parallel and distributed implementations are usually targeted to solve larger problems involving larger ANNs and larger data sets.

There are two major parallelization trends for FFANNs, the network-partitioning approach and the pattern-partitioning approach. In the former, network operations are partitioned among different processors. This trend represents a form of fine-grained parallelism. In the latter, the training data set is distributed among processors while keeping a complete copy of the whole network in each processor. This trend represents a form of coarse-grained parallelism that is suitable only if the data set is much larger in comparison to the network size.

Supervised training is used to adjust the network weights using training data set. This is a repetitive process of presenting the training data to the network's input and then determine the error between the actual output and the intended target output. There are two major training paradigms, the trajectory-driven, based on the mathematical gradient calculations, and the evolutionary-based training, a stochastic global optimization technique inspired from biological and physical processes. The former is known for its tendency to converge to a local solution that is not global. Many variant methods exist for each of these paradigms. Evolutionary-based methods incorporate using some sort of fitness function derived from the error calculation functions, a data representation and a termination condition. These methods are either used to evolve network weights, structure (topology and parameters) or both.

The price-to-performance ratio of commodity computers equipped with GPUs has attracted many within the high-performance computing community. ANN computations can be expressed as a set of matrix operations and GPUs are highly optimized to perform such kind of operations. ANN applications utilizing such GPUs have reported impressive speedups in comparison with the CPU only counterparts. However, GPU programming is still substantially more difficult and requires more effort than developing CPU multithreaded applications.

REFERENCES

Abraham, A. (2004). Meta learning evolutionary artificial neural networks. *Neurocomputing,* 56, pp.1-38.

Al-Jaroodi, J., Mohamed, N., Jiang, H. & Swanson, D. (2003). Modeling parallel applications performance on heterogeneous systems. *Proceedings of the International Parallel and Distributed Processing Symposium (IPDPS'03), 22-26 April, Nice, France.*

Alba, E. & Chicano, J.F. (2004). Training neural networks with ga hybrid algorithms. *Genetic and evolutionary computation (gecco 2004).* Springer Berlin / Heidelberg, pp.852-863.

Albuquerque, A.R.P.L. (1994). The adherence of the object oriented programming paradigm on the simulation of artificial neural networks. *IEEE International Conference on Neural Networks, June 27-29, Florida, USA.* IEEE. pp.3900-3904.

Anderson, J.A., Lorenz, C.D. & Travesset, A. (2008). General purpose molecular dynamics simulations fully implemented on graphics processing units. *Journal of Computational Physics,* 227 (10), pp.5342-5359.

Atanasov, D. (2005). General purpose gpu programming. *IN: International Conference on Computer Systems and Technologies – CompSysTech'2005, 16-17 June, Varna, Bulgaria.* pp.V.11-1 - V.11.6.

Bascil, M.S. & Temurtas, F. (2009). A study on hepatitis disease diagnosis using multilayer neural network with levenberg marquardt training algorithm. *Journal of Medical Systems* [online].

Bishop, C.M. (1999). *Pattern recognition and feed-forward networks.* MIT Press.

Blum, C. (2005). Ant colony optimization: Introduction and recent trends. *Physics of Life Reviews*, 2, pp.353-373.

Blum, C. & Socha, K. (2005). Training feed-forward neural networks with ant colony optimization: An application to pattern classification. *IN: Fifth International Conference on Hybrid Intelligent Systems (HIS '05), 6 - 9 November, Rio de Janeiro, Brazil.* p.6.

Bochev, V. (1993). Distributed arithmetic implementation of artificial neural networks. *IEEE Transactions on Signal Processing,* 41 (5), pp.2010-2013.

Calvert, D. & Guan, J. (2005). Distributed artificial neural network architectures. *Proceedings of the 19th International Symposium on High Performance Computing Systems and Applications (HPCS'05), Guelph, Ontario.* pp.2-10.

Caruana, R., Lawrence, S. & Giles, C.L. (2000). Overfitting in neural nets: Backpropagation, conjugate gradient, and early stopping. *IN: Neural Information Processing Systems Conference, Denver, CO, USA.* pp.402-408.

Cetişli, B. & Barkana, A. (2010). Speeding up the scaled conjugate gradient algorithm and its application in neuro-fuzzy classifier training. *Soft Computing,* 14, pp.365-378.

Che, S., Boyer, M., Meng, J., Tarjan, D., Sheaffer, J.W. & Skadron, K. (2008). A performance study on general-purpose applications on graphics processors using cuda. *Journal of Parallel and Distributed Computing,* 68, pp.1370-1380.

Chronopoulos, A.T. & Sarangapani, J. (2002). A distributed discrete-time neural network architecture for pattern allocation and control. *Proceedings of the International Parallel and Distributed Processing Symposium (IPDPS'02), Florida, USA.* IEEE Computer Society. pp.204-211.

Conforth, M. & Meng, Y. (2008). Reinforcement learning for neural networks using swarm intelligence. *IN: Swarm Intelligence Symposium (SIS 2008), 21-23 September, St. Louis, Missouri, USA.* IEEE, pp.1-7.

Debes, K., Koenig, A. & Gross, H.-M. (2005). Transfer functions in artificial neural networks - a simulation-based tutorial. *Brains, Minds and Media,* 2005 (bmm151).

Delgado, M., Pegalajar, M.C. & Cuellar, M.P. (2006). Memetic evolutionary training for recurrent neural networks: An application to time-series prediction. *Expert Systems,* 23 (2), pp.99-115.

Dennis, J.E. & Schnabel, R.B. (1983). *Numerical methods for unconstrained optimization and nonlinear equations.* New Jersey: Prentice-Hall.

Dolan, R. & DeSouza, G. (2009). Gpu-based simulation of cellular neural networks for image processing. *Proceedings of International Joing Conference on Neural Networks, 14-19 June, Atlanta, Georgia, USA.* IEEE. pp.730-735.

Dorigo, M., Maniezzo, V. & Colorni, A. (1996). Ant system: Optimization by a colony of cooperating agents. *IEEE Transactions on Systems, Man, and Cybernetics,* 26 (Part B), pp.29-41.

Dorsey, R.E., Johnson, J.D. & Mayer, W.J. (1994). A genetic algoirthm for the training of feedforward neural networks. *Advances in A.pngicial Intelligence in Economics, Finance, and Management* 1,pp.93-111.

Duch, W. & Jankowski, N. (2000). Taxonomy of neural transfer functions. *International Joint Conference on Neural Networks (IJCNN 2000), Como, Italy.* IEEE. pp.477-482.

Duren, R.W., Marks II, R.J. & Reynolds, P.D. (2007). Real-time neural network inversion on the src-6e reconfigurable computer. *IEEE TRANSACTIONS ON NEURAL NETWORKS,* 18 (3), pp.889-901.

Eberhart, R.C. & Kennedy, J. (1995). A new optimizer using particle swarm theory. *Proceedings of the Sixth International Symposium on Micro Machine and Human Science, Nagoya, Japan.* pp.39-43.

Eiben, A.E. & Smith, J.E. (2008). *Introduction to evolutionary computing.* New York: Springer.

El Emam, K., Khalafalla, F.B., Hoptroff, R.G. & Hall, T.J. (1991). Object oriented neural networks. *IN: International Conference on Control 1991. (Control'91), 25-28 March,* pp.1007-1010.

Factor, M., Schuster, A. & Shagin, K. (2004). A distributed runtime for java: Yesterday and today. *IN: Proceedings of the 18th International Parallel and Distributed Processing Symposium (IPDPS'04), 26-30 April, Santa Fe, New Mexico.* p.159.

Fausett, L. (1994). *Fundamentals of neural networks architectures, algorithms, and applications.* New Jersey: Prentice Hall.

Ferentinos, K.P. (2005). Biological engineering applications of feedforward neural networks designed and parameterized by genetic algorithms. *Neural Networks,* 18, pp.934-950.

Ferrer, D., Gonz´alez, R., Fleitas, R., Acle, J.P.e. & Canetti, R. (2004). Neurofpga - implementing artificial neural networks on programmable logic devices. *Proceedings of the Design, Automation and Test in Europe Conference and Exhibition Designers' Forum (DATE'04), 16-20 February, Paris, France.* IEEE Computer Society. pp.218-223.

Fiesler, E. & Beale, R. (1996). Neural network topologies. *Handbook of neural computation.*

Fiesler, E. & Fulcher, J. (1994). Neural network classification and formalization. *Computer Standards & Interfaces,* 16 (3), pp.231-239.

Fish, K.E., Johnson, J.D., Dorsey, R.E. & Blodgett, J.G. (2004). Using an artificial neural network trained with a genetic algorithm to model brand share *Journal of Business Research,* 57 (1), pp.79-85.

Freeman, T.L. & Phillips, C. (1992). *Parallel numerical algorithms.* Prentice Hall.

Fujita, O. (1998). Statistical estimation of the number of hidden units for feedforward neural networks. *Neural Networks,* 11, pp.851-859.

Gao, W. (2008). Evolutionary neural network based on new ant colony algorithm. *IN: International Symposium on Computational Intelligence and Design (ISCID '08), 17-18 October, Wuhan, China.* pp.318 - 321.

Geem, Z.W. (2003). Window-based decision support system for the water pipe condition assessment using artificial neural network. *Proceedings of 2003 Conference of the Environmental and Water Resources Institute, 23-26 June, Philadelphia, PA, USA.* ASCE. pp.2027-2032.

Geem, Z.W., Kim, J.H. & Loganathan, G.V. (2002). Application of harmony search algorithm to water resources problems. *Proceedings of 2002 Conference of the Environmental and Water Resources Institute, 19-22 May, Roanoke, VA, USA.* ASCE, CDROM. pp.1-9.

Geem, Z.W. & Roper, W.E. (2009). Energy demand estimation of south korea using artificial neural networks. *Energy Policy,* 37, pp.4049-4054.

Geem, Z.W., Tseng, C.-L., Kim, J. & Bae, C. (2007). Trenchless water pipe condition assessment using artificial neural network. *Proceedings of the International Pipeline Conference (Pipelines 2007), 8-11 July, Boston, MA, USA.* ASCE. pp.1-9.

Geethanjali, M., Slochanal, S.M.R. & Bhavani, R. (2008). Pso trained ann-based differential protection scheme for power transformers. *Neurocomputing,* 71, pp.904-918.

Goetz, B., Peierls, T., Bloch, J., Bowbeer, J., Holmes, D. & Lea, D. (2006). *Java concurrency in practice.* Addison-Wesley Professional.

Guijarro-Berdinas, B., Fontenla-Romero, O., Perez-Sanchez, B. & Alonso-Betanzos, A. (2006). A new initialization method for neural networks using sensitivity analysis. *IN: International Conference on Mathematical and Statistical Modeling, Ciudad Real, Spain.* pp.1-9.

Gupta, J.N.D. & Sexton, R.S. (1999). Comparing backpropagation with a genetic algorithm for neural network training. *Omega, The International Journal of Management Science,* 27 (1999), pp.679-684.

Hagan, M.T., Demuth, H.B. & Beale, M.H. (1996). *Neural network design.* Boston, MA: PWS Publishing.

Hagan, M.T. & Menhaj, M. (1994). Training feedforward networks with the marquardt algorithm. *IEEE Transactions on Neural Networks*, 5 (6), pp.989-993.

Hamey, L.G.C. (1998). Xor has no local minima: A case study in neural network error surface analysis. *Neural Networks*, 11, pp.669-681.

Hassoun, M.H. (1995). *Fundamentals of artificial neural networks*. Massachusetts: MIT Press, Cambridge.

Hereld, M., Stevens, R.L., van Drongelen, W. & Lee, H.C. (2004). Developing a petascale neural simulation. *Proceedings of the 26th Annual International Conference of the IEEE EMBS, 1-5 September, San Francisco, CA, USA*. pp.3999-4002.

Hill, M.D. & Marty, M.R. (2008). Amdahl's law in the multicore era. *Computer*, 41 (7), pp.33-38.

Ho, T.-Y., Lam, P.-M. & Leung, C.-S. (2008). Parallelization of cellular neural networks on gpu. *Pattern Recognition*, 41 (8), pp.2684-2692.

Holland, J. (1975). *Adaptation in natural and artificial systems*. University of Michigan Press.

Howlett, R.J. & Walters, S.D. (1999). Multi-computer neural networks architecture. *Electronics Letters*, 35 (16), pp.1350-1352.

Huang, C.-Y., Chen, L.-H., Chen, Y.-L. & Chang, F.M. (2009). Evaluating the process of a genetic algorithm to improve the back-propagation network: A monte carlo study. *Expert Systems with Applications*, 36 (2009), pp.1459-1465.

Huang, N.-F., Hung, H.-W., Lai, S.-H., Chu, Y.-M. & Tsai, W.-Y. (2008). A gpu-based multiple-pattern matching algorithm for network intrusion detection systems. *IN: 22nd International Conference on Advanced Information Networking and Applications (AINA 2008), Ginowan city, Okinawa, Japan*. IEEE Computer Society, pp.62-67.

Iyer, M.S. & Rhinehart, R.R. (2000). A novel method to stop neural network training. *Proceedings of the American Control Conference, 28-30 June, Chicago, Illinois*. pp.929-933.

Jang, H., Park, A. & Jung, K. (2008). Neural network implementation using cuda and openmp. *IN: Digital Image Computing: Techniques and Applications (DICTA '08), 1-3 December, Canberra, Australia*. IEEE Computer Society, pp.155-161.

Jayalakshmi, T. & Santhakumaran, A. (2010). Improved gradient descent back propagation neural networks for diagnoses of type ii diabetes mellitus. *Global Journal of Computer Science and Technology*, 9 (5).

Jiang, X. & Wah, A.H.K.S. (2003). Constructing and training feed-forwardneural networks for pattern classifcation. *Pattern Recognition,* 36, pp.853-867.

Johansson, C. & Lansner, A. (2006). Towards cortex sized artificial neural systems. *Neural Networks,* 20 (1), pp.48-61.

Jung, S. & Kim, S.s. (2007). Hardware implementation of a real-time neural network controller with a dsp and an fpga for nonlinear systems. *IEEE Transactions on Industrial Electronics,* 54 (1), pp.265-271.

Junyou, B. (2007). Stock price forecasting using pso-trained neural networks. *IN: IEEE Congress on Evolutionary Computation (CEC 2007) 25-28 September, Singapore.* IEEE, pp.2879-2885.

Kathirvalavakumar, T. & Thangavel, P. (2006). A modified backpropagation training algorithm for feedforward neural networks. *Neural Processing Letters,* 23, pp.111-119.

Kattan, A., Abdullah, R. & Salam, R.A. (2006). Java: From "Hard coding" To using an integrated development environment. *IN: The 2nd International Conference on Distributed Frameworks for Multimedia Applications (DFMA'06), Penang, Malaysia.* pp.1 - 6.

Kattan, A., Abdullah, R. & Salam, R.A. (2009a). Reducing feed-forward neural network processing time utilizing matrix multiplication algorithms on heterogeneous distributed systems. *IN: First International Conference on Computational Intelligence, Communication Systems and Networks (CICSYN '09), 23-25 July, Indore, India.* IEEE Computer Society, pp.431 - 435.

Kattan, A., Abdullah, R. & Salam, R.A. (2009b). A survey on neural network implementation techniques from a parallel and distributed perspective. *IN: Malaysian Joint Conference on Artificial Intelligence (MJCAI2009), 14-16 July, Kuala Lumpur, Malaysia.*

Kattan, A., Abdullah, R. & Salam, R.A. (2010). Training feed-forward neural networks using a parallel genetic algorithm with the best must survive strategy. *IN: International Conference on Intelligent Systems, Modelling and Simulation (ISMS 2010), 27-29 January, Liverpool, UK.* IEEE Computer Society pp.96-99.

Kattan, A., Abdullah, R., Salam, R.A. & Ramadass, S. (2009a). Building distributed heterogeneous smart phone java applications; an evaluation from a development perspective. *Journal of Information and Communication Technology,* 8, pp.67-83.

Kattan, A., Abdullah, R., Salam, R.A. & Ramadass, S. (2009b). Towards developing distributed heterogeneous mobile phone applications. *IN:*

International Conference on Computing & Informatics (ICOCI09), 24-25 June, Kuala Lumpur, Malaysia. Universiti Utara Malaysia.

Kim, D., Kim, H. & Chung, D. (2005). A modified genetic algorithm for fast training neural networks. *Advances in neural networks - isnn 2005.* Springer Berlin / Heidelberg, pp.660-665.

Kiranyaz, S., Ince, T., Yildirim, A. & Gabbouj, M. (2009). Evolutionary artificial neural networks by multi-dimensional particle swarm optimization. *Neural Networks,* 22, pp.1448-1462.

Kostopoulos, A.E. & Grapsa, T.N. (2009). Self-scaled conjugate gradient training algorithms. *Neurocomputing,* 72, pp.3000-3019.

Koutsogiannakis, G., Savva, M. & Chang, J.M. (2002). Performance studies of remote method invocation in java. *IN: 21st IEEE International Performance, Computing, and Communications Conference, 3-5 April,* pp.1 - 8

Lane, K.M. & Neidinger, R.D. (1995). Neural networks from idea to implementation. *ACM Sigapl APL Quote Quad,* 25 (3), pp.27-37.

Lawrence, S. & Giles, C.L. (2000). Overfitting and neural networks: Conjugate gradient and backpropagation. *Proceedings of the IEEE-INNS-ENNS International Joint Conference on Neural Networks (IJCNN 2000), 24-27 July, Como, Italy.* IEEE. pp.114-119.

Liang, F. (2007). Annealing stochastic approximation monte carlo algorithm for neural network training. *Mach Learn,* 68, pp.201-233.

Liu, Y., Starzyk, J.A. & Zhu, Z. (2008). Optimized approximation algorithm in neural networks without overfitting. *IEEE Transactions on Neural Networks,* 19 (6), pp.983-995.

Marini, F., Magri, A.L. & Bucci, R. (2007). Multilayer feed-forward artificial neural networks for class modeling. *Chemometrics and intelligent laboratory systems,* 88, pp.118-124.

Marziale, L., Richard III, G.G. & Roussev, V. (2007). Massive threading: Using gpus to increase the performance of digital forensics tools. *Digital Investigation,* 4 (Supplement 1), pp.73-81.

Mathia, K. & Clark, J. (2002). On neural network hardware and programming paradigms. *IN: Proceedings of the 2002 International Joint Conference on Neural Networks (IJCNN '02), 12-17 May, Hawaii, USA.* pp.2692-2697.

McCormick, P., Inman, J., Ahrens, J., Mohd-Yusof, J., Roth, G. & Cummins, S. (2008). Scout: A data-parallel programming language for graphics processors. *Parallel Computing,* 33 (10-11), pp.648-622.

Mehrotra, P., Venlcatesan, R. & Quaicoe, J.E. (1997). Development of a flexible object-oriented artificial neural network simulator. *IEEE 1997*

Canadian Conference on Electrical and Computer Engineering (CCECE'97), May 25-28, Vancouver, Canada. IEEE. pp.318-321.

Meuth, R.J. & Wunsch II, D.C. (2007). A survey of neural computation on graphics processing hardware. *IN: IEEE 22nd International Symposium on Intelligent Control (ISIC 2007) 1-3 October, Singapore.* IEEE, pp.524-527.

Milea, C. & Slvasta, P. (2001). Using distributed neural networks in automated optical inspection. *IN: 24th International Spring Seminar on Electronics Technology, 5-9 May, Calimanesti-Caciula.ta, Romania.* pp.286-288.

Moerland, P., Fiesler, E. & Beale, R. (1997). Neural network adaptations to hardware implementations. *Handbook of neural computation.* Oxford University Press, pp.E1.2:1-13.

Montana, D.J. (1995). Neural network weight selection using genetic algorithms. *Intelligent Hybrid Systems*, pp.85-104.

Montana, D.J. & Davis, L. (1989). Training feedforward neural networks using genetic algorithms. *Proceedings of the International Joint Conference on Artificial Intelligence, August 20-25, Detroit, USA.* p762.

Moraga, C. (2007). Design of neural networks. *Knowledge-based intelligent information and engineering systems.* Springer Berlin/Heidelberg, pp.26-33.

Mullen, R.J., Monekosso, D., Barman, S. & Remagnino, P. (2009). A review of ant algorithms. *Expert Systems with Applications,* 36, pp.9608-9617.

Nasir, M.L., John, R.I. & Bennett, S.C. (2000). Predicting corporate bankruptcy using artificial neural networks. *Journal of Applied Accounting Research,* 5 (3), pp.30-52.

Nasr, M.b. & Chtourou, M. (2006). A hybrid training algorithm for feedforward neural networks *Neural Processing Letters,* 24, pp.107-117.

Oh, I.-S. & Suen, C.Y. (2002). A class-modular feedforward neural network for handwriting recognition. *Pattern Recognition,* 35, pp.229-244.

Oh, K.-S. & Jung, K. (2004). Gpu implementation of neural networks. *Pattern Recognition,* 37 (6), pp.1311-1314.

Padhy, N.P. (2005). *Artificial intelligence and intelligent systems.* 1st ed. Delhi: Oxford University Press.

Palmes, P.P. & Usui, S. (2005). Robustness, evolvability, and optimality of evolutionary neural networks. *Bio Systems,* 82, pp.168-188.

Pandey, S.N., Tapaswi, S. & Srivastava, L. (2010). Integrated evolutionary neural network approach with distributed computing for congestion management. *Applied Soft Computing,* 10, pp.251-260.

Rocha, M., Cortez, P. & Neves, J. (2007). Evolution of neural networks for classification and regression. *Neurocomputing,* 70, pp.2809-2816.

Rogers, J. (1997). *Object-oriented neural networks in c++.* San Diego, California: Academic Press, An Imprint of Elsevier.

Rosin, P.L. & Fierens, F. (1995). Improving neural network generalisation. *IN: Geoscience and Remote Sensing Symposium (IGARSS '95), 10-14 July, Florence, Italy.* IEEE, pp.1255 - 1257.

Ruf, B. & Schmitt, M. (1998). Self-organization of spiking neurons using action potential timing. *IEEE TRANSACTIONS ON NEURAL NETWORKS,* 9 (3), pp.575-578.

Seiffert, U. (2004). Artificial neural networks on massively parallel computer hardware. *Neurocomputing,* 57, pp.135-150.

Sexton, R.S. & Dorsey, R.E. (2000). Reliable classification using neural networks: A genetic algorithm and backpropagation comparison. *Decision Support Systems,* 30 (1), pp.11-22.

Sexton, R.S., Dorsey, R.E. & Jhonson, J.D. (1998). Towards global optimization of neural networks: A comparison of the genetic algorithm and backpropagation. *Decision Support Systems,* 22, pp.171-185.

Sexton, R.S., Dorsey, R.E. & Sikander, N.A. (2004). Simultaneous optimization of neural network function and architecture algorithm. *Decision Support Systems,* 30 (1), pp.11-22.

Shi, H. & Li, W. (2009). Artificial neural networks with ant colony optimization for assessing performance of residential buildings. *IN: International Conference on Future BioMedical Information Engineering (FBIE 2009), 13-14 December,* IEEE, pp.379-382.

Siddique, M.N.H. & Tokhi, M.O. (2001). Training neural networks: Backpropagation vs. Genetic algorithms. *International Joint Conference on Neural Networks (IJCNN '01), 15-19 July, Washington, DC* pp.2673 - 2678.

Siwei, L. (2000). The implementation of a neurocomputing environment based on a network of heterogeneous computers. *5th International Conference on Signal Processing (WCCC-ICSP 2000), August, Beijing, China.* IEEE. pp.1679-1683.

Skapura, D.M. (1996). *Building neural networks.* New York: ACM Press.

Škutova, J. (2008). Weights initialization methods for mlp neural networks. *Transactions of the VŠB,* LIV, article No. 1636 (2), pp.147-152.

Soliman, M.I. & Mohamed, S.A. (2008). A highly efficient implementation of a backpropagation learning algorithm using matrix isa. *Journal of Parallel and Distributed Computing,* 68, pp.949–961.

Strey, A. (2004). A comparison of openmp and mpi for neural network simulations on a sunfire 6800. *Advances in Parallel Computing*, 13, pp.201-208.

Svozil, D., Kvasnicka, V. & Pospichal, J. (1997). Introduction to multi-layer feed-forward neural networks. *Chemometrics and intelligent laboratory systems*, 39, pp.43-62.

Sykes, E.R. & Mirkovic, A. (2005). A fully parallel and scalable implementation of a hopfield neural network on the sharc-net supercomputer. *IN: 19th International Symposium on High Performance Computing Systems and Applications (HPCS 2005), 15-18 May, Ontario, Canada.* pp.103-109.

Teoh, E.J., Tan, K.C. & Xiang, C. (2006). Estimating the number of hidden neurons in a feedforward network using the singular value decomposition. *IEEE Transactions on Neural Networks*, 17 (6), pp.1623-1629

Teschl, R., Randeu, W.L. & Teschl, F. (2007). Improving weather radar estimates of rainfall using feed-forward neural networks. *Neural Networks*, 20, pp.519-527.

Thorpe, S., Delorme, A. & Van Rullen, R. (2001). Spike-based strategies for rapid processing. *Neural Networks*, 14, pp.715-725.

Tsuchiyama, R., Nakamura, T., Iizuka, T., Asahara, A. & Miki, S. (2010). *The opencl programming book (kindle edition).* First Edition ed. Tokyo: Fixstars Corporation.

Valentini, G. & Masulli, F. (2002). Neurobjects: An object-oriented library for neural network development. *Neurocomputing*, 48, pp.623-646.

Wang, X., Hou, Z.-G., Zou, A., Tan, M. & Cheng, L. (2008). A behavior controller based on spiking neural networks for mobile robots. *Neurocomputing*, 71 (4-6), pp.655-666.

Wei, G. (2007). Study on evolutionary neural network based on ant colony optimization. *IN: International Conference on Computational Intelligence and Security Workshops, 15-19 Dec, Harbin, Heilongjiang, China.* pp.3-6.

Wueng, M.-C., Yang, F.-F. & Yang, C.-Z. (2004). A novel java rmi middleware design for active networks. *IN: IEEE Region 10 Conference (TENCON 2004), 21-24 Nov*, pp.68-71.

Yao, X. (1993). A review of evolutionary artificial neural networks. *International Journal of Intelligent Systems*, 8 (4), pp.539-567.

Yu, J., Wang, S. & Xi, L. (2008). Evolving artificial neural networks using an improved pso and dpso. *Neurocomputing*, 71, pp.1054-1060.

Yuan, H.C., Xiong, F.L. & Huai, X.Y. (2003). A method for estimating the number of hidden neurons in feed-forward neural networks based on information entropy. *Computers and Electronics in Agriculture,* 40, pp.57-64.

Zhang, Y. & Wu, L. (2008). Weights optimization of neural networks via improved bco approach. *Progress In Electromagnetics Research,* 83, pp.185-198.

Zhou, J., Duan, Z., Li, Y., Deng, J. & Yu, D. (2006). Pso-based neural network optimization and its utilization in a boring machine. *Journal of Materials Processing Technology,* 178, pp.19-23.

INDEX